Singing in the o of not

Critical praise for Djelloul Marbrook's poetry

Far from Algiers (2008, Kent State University Press)

... as succinct as most stanzas by Dickinson... an unusually mature, confidently composed first poetry collection.

—Susanna Roxman, *Prairie Schooner*
(author of *Crossing the North Sea*)

... brings together the energy of a young poet with the wisdom of long experience.

—Edward Hirsch, Guggenheim Foundation

... honors a lifetime of hidden achievement.

—Toi Derricotte, Wick Award judge

... wise and flinty poems outfox the Furies of exile, prejudice, and longing... a remarkable and distinctive debut.

—Cyrus Cassells, National Poetry Series winner

Brash Ice (2014, Leaky Boot Press, UK)

... resonates with wisdom and a keen eye for the beautiful things of this world ...a poetry that would make brash ice melt again.

—George Drew, author of *The View From Jackass Hill*

... a precision that occasionally recalls Yeats ...

—James Polk, *The Country and Abroad*

... aesthetically pleasing, thematically intriguing ...

—Michael Young, *The Poetry*

Brushstrokes and glances (2010, Deerbrook Editions)

Whether it is commentary on state power, corporate greed, or the intensely personal death of a loved one, Djelloul Marbrook is clear sighted, eloquent, and precise. As the title of the collection suggests, he uses the lightest touch, a collection of fragments, brushstrokes and glances, to fashion poems that resonate with truth and honesty.

—Phil Constable, *New York Journal of Books*

... looks at art the way a drinker drinks—deeply, passionately, and desperately, as if his life depended on it ... makes you want to run out to your favorite museum and look again, as you have never looked before, until the lights go out.

—Barbara Louise Ungar, author of *Thrift; Charlotte Bronte, You Ruined My Life; The Origin of the Milky Way*

... one of those colossal poets able to bridge worlds—poetry and art, heart and mind—with rare wit, grace, and sincerity; a soft-spoken artist with the courage to face the "fatal beckoning" of his muse ... crisp intellect, seamlessly interwoven with loss and longing. ... poetry at its best: at once both gritty and refined, private and political, tender and tough as iron ... well worth reading."

—Michael Meyerhofer, author of *What to do if you're buried alive*, *Damnatio Memoriae*, *Blue Collar Eulogies*

...delicately wrought... highly recommended reading...because, ultimately, this witness so clearly loves his subject.

—Eileen Tabios, Editor, *Galatea Resurrects*

Riding Thermals to Winter Grounds (2017, Leaky Boot)

... some very powerful lines, such as: "And then, near the end of my life, I become the man I wanted to be without the fuss and bother of giving a damn."

—Sidney Grayling, Editor, Onager Editions

☙

Critical praise for Djelloul Marbrook's fiction

Guest Boy (2018, Leaky Boot)

What Marbrook does so well in *Guest Boy* is the contradictory elegance he showed in *Saraceno*. He finds the tender and poetic heart of very tough men. In *Saraceno*, it was low-level mobsters; in *Guest Boy*, it's men of the sea. They're a horny-handed bunch, and Marbrook's familiarity with ships and the characters of mean-street ports is deep and exciting. But Marbrook knows that these guys have a lot more going on within, and are simultaneously deeply tender philosophers. It's a mesmerizing book... You'll find yourself thinking about it long after you've finished reading.

—Dan Baum, author of *Gun Guys* (2013), *Nine Lives* (2009), and others

Guest Boy is a complex work: deep, passionate, exciting and beautifully written with flashbacks and imagery merging real and surreal. By opening up routes to the culture and history of the Arab world, *Guest Boy* helps us understand that world and our own.

—Sanford Fraser, author of *Tourist* and *Among Strangers I've Known All My Life*

... it is in books like this that I seek answers and guidance as I travel my own path to enlightenment and contentment. This book opened a struggle in me...

—Isla McKetta, editor, *A Geography of Reading*

Artemisia's Wolf (title story, *A Warding Circle*, 2017, Leaky Boot)

...Djelloul Marbrook's impressive novella...successfully blends humor and satire (and perhaps even a touch of magic realism) into its short length...an engrossing story, but what might strike the reader most throughout the book is its infusion of breathtaking poetry...a stunning rebuke to notoriously misogynist subcultures like the New York art scene, showing us just how hard it is for a young woman to be judged on her creative talent alone.

—Tommy Zurhellen, *Hudson River Valley Review*

...lets his powerful imagination run wild, leading the fiction into unexpected corners where weird performers hold court and produce endings that both astonish and are frequently magical.

—James Polk, *The Country and Abroad*, former contributing editor of *Art/World*.

Saraceno

Djelloul Marbrook writes dialogue that not only entertains with an intoxicating clickety-clack, but also packs a truth about low-life mob culture "The Sopranos" only hints at. You can practically smell the anisette and filling-station coffee.

—Dan Baum, author of *Gun Guys* (2013), *Nine Lives: Mystery, Magic, Death and Life in New Orleans* (2009), and others

...a good ear for crackling dialogue... I love Marbrook's crude, raw music of the streets. The notes are authentic and on target...

—Sam Coale, *The Providence* (RI) *Journal*

...an entirely new variety of gangster tale... a Mafia story sculpted with the most refined of sensibilities from the clay of high art and philosophy... the kind of writer I take real pleasure in discovering...a mature artist whose rich body of work is finally coming to light.

—Brent Robison, editor, *Prima Materia*

Alice Miller's Room
(title story, *Making Room*, 2017, Leaky Boot)

This enchanting novella is a delicately wrought homage to Jung's famous principle of meaningful coincidence...

—*Breakfast All Day*, UK

...the story draws us into that mysterious and terrifying realm where the heart will have its say and all who enter leave transformed...

—Dr. Patricia L. Divine, Head Start program lifetime service award winner

Mean Bastards Making Nice (2014, Leaky Boot)

I love it. I admire it. It is you at your best.

—Novelist Gail Godwin on "The Pain of Wearing Our Faces"

Singing in the o of not

poems by

Djelloul Marbrook

LEAKY BOOT PRESS

Singing in the o of not
by Djelloul Marbrook

Acknowledgments

"Bedfellows" was published in *Le Zaparogue* (Denmark) in 2014

First published in 2019 by
Leaky Boot Press
http://www.leakyboot.com

Copyright © 2019 Djelloul Marbrook
All rights reserved

No part of this book may be reproduced or transmitted in any form or by any means, electronic, mechanical, photocopying, recording, or otherwise, without prior written permission of the author.

ISBN: 978-1-909849-59-4

Author's Acknowledgments

Endless thanks are owed to my wife, Marilyn, who has in so many ways made all my work possible; to James Goddard, my publisher, whose steadfast faith in my work brought it to light and buoyed me in rough waters; to Sebastien Doubinsky, who published my work and introduced me to James Goddard; to Brent Robison, whose wizardly videos and deft hand with e-books still astonish me; to Kevin Swanwick, whose radiance as a reader and advisor unfailingly enlightens me; and to Emily Brooks, whose artistic taste, good cheer and resourcefulness seem fathomless.

for Andrew Franck, dear friend

*He saw the lightning in the east and longed for the east,
but if it had flashed in the west he would have longed for the west.
My desire is for the lightning and its gleam, not for the places and the earth.*

—Ibn al-'Arabi

Blue ampersand

*Kill me, skin whispers
to arctic bone,
I'm finished
with this disguise.*

*Blue ampersand,
sere caul scuttling
through the snowy street
to the frozen river:
alluding to friends.*

—DM

Contents

Proem
No one cloaked in clothes — 21

The abandoned station
My death of cold — 25
If in some cracked window — 26
For whom my silence was — 31
Sober but for angels — 32
Desk in this other world — 34
His feet hate each other — 35
Eidolon — 36
Creatures from whom I was torn — 38
Last things ripening — 39
What I cobble rots — 40

Lost in the o of not
A new kind of zero — 43
Oh — 45
The word not — 46
To cope with treason — 47
When I'm my shadow — 48
To kill but not to harm — 49

Chaos	50
Escaping them	51
Consequence aside	52
Loss	53
Dry bones in their cars	54
Outfall	55
As if they had a conscience	56
Infinite ampersand	57
The full intent of the reckless eye	58
To catch a lightning bolt	59
Under the bed	60

If one white wing

Bedfellows	63
Atoms & evenings	64
The heronry	65
Hadrian weeps	66
Lioness in the rug	68
The chef is full of it	69
Hurt of golems	70
Inheritance	72
Riding alligators	73
Cosmos trickling down	74
This abandoner of dogs	75
Dusty phones	76
Cyberspace	77
Old artist	78

Gerund, goodbye

Trinity of spies	81
Gerund, goodbye	82
All that makes him laugh	84

Wardrobes of Numina	85
Her face	86
Carbon mnemonic	87
Consent to ash	88
The edible curd of a question mark	89
Tag	90
Goodbye beasts	91
Furnace of red lilies	92
Fit to walk naked	93
The light is too bright	94
All he had to say	95

Proem

No one cloaked in clothes

Sing, burglar, sing to the unseen,
to no one cloaked in clothes,
to vast unbelonging,
not longing to complain
but to consort
with shapeless ones
for whom to name is to disdain.

Sing yourself inside out—
elementals hear you,
angels, devas, daemons, creatures
who depend upon your words
to sing cities into being,
to christen perilous thought.

Sing yourself into a panther,
meteor-eyed and bounding
star to star ravening
to limn aeons' worth of dreams.

Sing, intruder, not to be seen
or even to be remembered
but to complete a holy circuit
of companions longing for you
in the etheric of your fingertips.

Sing, saboteur, to water
thyme-delirious greenswards
and white woods of heaven,
to celebrate the eye of zero,
to vanish in it.

The abandoned station

My death of cold

I think I've caught my death of cold,
a better word for whatever it is,
and am not as afraid of language now
as when I didn't know it was nostalgia
for one lost home or another, lament,
a lost poetics which if remembered
might free me from what's closing in
which for convenience's sake I call
my death of cold, knowing more
than I've ever been willing to say,
seeing more than is safe to admit.
It's going to act like other things,
but I know when it got into my bones
and in my old age I smile and call it
sudden infant death syndrome or
how about failure to thrive?

If in some cracked window

I

Notes he never could sing,
shading, color, interval,
songs that eluded him
summon a motley
to the abandoned station
at the arctic of the park
to celebrate the arrival
of the express to empathy
where the half-forgotten await
the arrival of yearnings postponed.

He smells of hyacinth,
not piss and disease.

Dogs sniff him and wag their tails,
but they are innocent.

The question is
will the gaffer watching him
in Antarctica
recognize his intent,
or muddle words with his toe,
and follow ripples
to their nether ends?

—eidolon, fylgia, wraith, fetch, doppelganger—

will the gaffer watching him
come to the station
up the whitening park?

His instrumental body plays
the lost or strangled tunes
as if they'd mastered him.

The passengers embark—
for whom does he send them on ahead,
the living or the dead?

Silent night, holy night,
so difficult to sing right.

Sotto voce as falling snow
this herald angel sings,
church bells murmur,
whistles hail
halfling's rest.

A dying man is truly blessed
if in some cracked window
he sees that all he wants
accompanies him.

This is his song,
impeccable and sweet
after years of croaking:
no one has anything I want,
not one of you second persons
who beguiled me, you
have become third persons
listening to songs on burner phones
picked from trash in parks
and that is not as sad as you think
because you're on the trail of a man
becoming something besides
a damned fool or an angel.

II

None of the three persons can tell what,
but it elicits song, melodies
whose slides once he couldn't handle.

Abandon with good will so eerie we
no longer trust things to hold their shape
or anything to be what we supposed.

We rush to the station lest
it be not there. This is apocalypse,
so help us God or not,
this listening to a man singing
of not needing,
least of all from us.

You missed the signal,
you wrapped it in your house flag,
and a thousand years later
you realized a dozen deaths
were hardly payment enough
for your inattention.

III

How may I help you?

Whatever it was you missed it
you chose to miss it,
went on fantasizing
as if nothing had happened
blowing another thousand years.

What do you know of nakedness?
The signal wasn't wrapped,
you fug-wrapped it
as the signaler knew you would.

What can I do for you?

What a pleasant surprise!
We have some specials today.
May I tell you about warranties?

How hard it is to live here.

You may order it online.
We have a platinum card
for old men in parks
singing as implausibly
as Aeneas founding Rome.

We have an 800 number.

Singing deaf as he is
because the signal awoke the child
and the child at last made his own welcome
in the ice memes of the park.

A childish urge
to hear star beasts breathe
becomes an ambition
to see them breed.

Our nether parts know better than mind
if we are welcome in the dark
but we prefer adjectives to verbs
to writhe ourselves around them.

Neither Iliad nor Odyssey convince
us not to stick around
and by setting out look what Aeneas
did for the Jews.

IV

He is broken up in the ways,
he hears puking in the alley,
shuffling of excruciants,
& had he been the guest of honor

he wouldn't be the one they came to see,
born as he was encased in a caul
wishing not to be seen.

Parties & funerals, flat-earth affairs,
his back is to the edge,
the door to quasars & black holes.
What are cities but ships' ways
to launch in the piss of gods?
He's always been in the ways
going to be broken on them.
Exits are not friends, enemies
pose as alternatives.
Somewhere someone inflates
to squeeze him out of room
and he responds as if he knows
it is this room and he must
appear to die to live & live
to disappear singing songs
he had no voice to sing before
in a tattered park among
vagrants in whose bosoms
he dies to sink.

For whom my silence was

    I sang my ode in silence.

    This is my after-song
    fading word repeated
    on blue lips,
    winter song
    of one convinced
    spring is for someone else,
    someone bolder, blessed,
    a favored one
    for whom my silence was
    and I will be
    a tributary
    of her navel
    observing the suave sweat, tic
    and testy look, getting in the way
    of adults with better things to do,
    higher stakes to play, watching
    too intent for the comfort
    of people who find witness
    an indecency, a biddable boy
    who puked in urinals not so much
    because of booze as bullshit.

Sober but for angels

Friendless but for angels,
the old drunk knows
sober's nothing to brag about.

His eyes stare
like the bottoms
of shot glasses.

The world is not a glad hand
of Cutty Sark,
tomorrow
no longer a swig
inducing a snarl
or a one-hour high
bludgeoned by the snark.

Friendless but for angels,
gone the bottle pickets,
the circus and the séance,
illusionists in a bottle.

He arranges yellow leaves
on a grate by a yellow curb,
he makes a paper ship
and launches it in sewers.

He wanted to get in,
to drink his way in
the wood, the bone, the glass,

to back-slap and shoot craps
only to find himself in
the company of angels
in the backrooms of his mind.

His camera is his friend,
in their communion
they worship rotting sills,
dandelions, loosestrife and thistle,
broken windows,
heaved-up graves.

Dry forty years,
drunk as he was born, he is
sober but for angels.

Desk in this other world

He's singing in the street.
From his breast pocket
I hear his heart's timpani,
motorcycle farts,
crossing signals, horns,
shouts and banging doors,
gingerliness of his feet,
choral laughter and complaint.

He's walking in the fire,
singing in the street,
entertaining presentiments
of transformation and ash,
singing to his breast pocket
to a world he's leaving,
a baby sobbing.

What's his smart phone doing here
on a desk in this other world?
What am I doing here sauntering
in shifty corridors unchallenged?
I thought them hornets and gnats,
moments behind me now
as I stand at the other end
of what? What do I need to know?

His feet hate each other

My feet trip each other, my brain tromps rue,
the message shudders in the king's hands,
the messenger waits to be shot, but for once
he is asked to sit and have a little wine,
and that is why on top of this I wobble
on the sunlight like a drunken dragon
flabbergasted by the triumph of truth.

I've been sitting this egg for eons never
dreaming messengers would come out alive
and head back to their dispatchers saying
he's thinking about it, can you imagine it?
It happens when the corridor is cleared
between the eye and the brain, which are made
of the same stuff, but usually the dragon

has gone home, the egg is left to the roc.
His feet hate each other, his brain threads rue.
Can a man stand this to happen in old age
that his delusions start to sing, that he pays out
rope to consequences, makes himself comfortable
in cemeteries and smells improbably honeyed
for an unclubbable chump shown out the back?

Eidolon

In the windows of the shut theater
we watch her face's light
sad to be so naked to us.
She knows we're outside
tiptoeing in condoms and cans
careful not to be seen,
more careful not to see
her bending light.

She never knows when her high notes
will open right-angle cracks
in the ceiling of someone's memory palace,
never knows when plaster will drop down
exposing interstices
where microbial empires thrive,
never knows when her bare feet
will step on someone's shattered glass
or when a bright urge to take offense
will poison wine with hellebore
and sling the song against the window.

She hears our tails scuttling
across assorted junk
as we return to our yammering place
having seen her naked
and not imagining she is sad
knowing we can't recover
the evil health we leave
under her window.

This time we brought a camera
to snag a loitering look,
to sell a broken slave
to a lascivious master
never guessing
her face depends upon its flesh
to hide the eidolon within
not from our camera's cruelty
but from an innocence
that could be consumed
by what it takes.

We may not be so concerned
but other creatures are
and that is why the cracks
should have warned us
trespass is upon ourselves.

Our choices about aperture,
shutter speed,
the quality of the lens,
the secrets of what we apprehend
tell us what we choose to see.

Leave her now to care
for the creatures we have left behind
under the shattered windows
of the cathedral of our fears.

Creatures from whom I was torn

behind lightfall in back of glass
a pavane of otherlings, whorls
sucking my tatters in until
nothing's left of what I had to do
but wings rushing in the night.

Creatures from whom I was torn
stare at me from behind reflections
on glass and I'm splattered
like blood on paintings
of the world behind me, thrown

like wine from the cups of revelers
at the pale of their dimension.
Nothing's left of what I had to do
not even the howl of my desire
to reunite behind lightfall
with the specters of my species.

Last things ripening

Undersea drinking water
will dry up
even before we reach it if
an old man gives up
studying the amplituhedron
to his despair
and we'll never know
what went wrong
because they carted his body
out of his flat before
he decided who anybody is
or what heroism is,
carted him out
just as he heard
last things ripening
to a winterkill of words.

What I cobble rots

Join rivet weld as I might
nothing holds but this calling
which we call love
because it withholds its name.

What I cobble rots,
corrodes, falls to ground,
is pecked away,
but what I let in soars

until I am jettisoned
and don't need a name
to see us on the bridge
still holding hands.

Lost in the o of not

A new kind of zero

The fulcrum of a moment in Albany
pulses under a leaf in Armenia
and nobody knows what's in the waitress's head
or her customer's. Assumptions
push drugs sure as doctors do for much
the same reason, and onlookers
should plant tulips in honor of what they don't know.
But then a hand lingers. All bets are off.
Religions go to bed. Shadows bolt.
And an unfamiliar light projects
our borrowed shapes on a painted wall.
Encounters threaten to erase us.
We wear our notions like Kevlar vests
against the hail of new ideas.
No more those intravenous adventures
in flashbacks doubling as emergency rooms.
No more universal donors arrested
when the light changes, hijackings
of strangers' reveries, fingerings
of cracks in studied demeanors.
No more measuring seismic shifts
in plates beneath magniloquence.
All that is given up to spume
off the cresting seas. We ride them
like pollen into parched hinterlands. Given up
to grandeur greater than place name,
pronoun, adverb, science—a calculus
waiting for a new kind of zero,

trembling on the fulcrum, shuddering,
a moment held in balance
too important to be revered.

Oh

I isolate one color with my camera
not to celebrate it but to see
where I am in relation to the rest.
It asks of me nothing but emptiness,
surrender. I emerge not speaking
of rewards or accomplishments,
I emerge lost in the oh of not.

The word not

You pick a little mortar out of the wall
not because you intend to repoint the brick
but because it felt like a loose cuticle or an itch
and then you find it was a cornerstone or a linchpin
and everything keeps tumbling down
because you couldn't leave one thing alone.

One thing after another comes out of the wall
that you depended on to keep eventuality out
and now each broken seal is a crisis
and there is no point in naming them
because one is as awful as another
and you see that the word not depends on a circle.

Somewhere there is this you who can stop
a thing from what it portends, stop
gerunds from molesting verbs
and each life is a longing for that you
which on the other side of things appears
as the holy wordlessness of dreams.

To cope with treason

Someone who cares not for . . .
haunts my photographs
scents my lens
times my shutter
turns white balance
to spectral shades.

As usual
I cope with treason
like a Medici prince
in service to art
playing someone who cares not for . . .
like a Lira da braccio.

When I'm my shadow

        Alive for another minute,
        hardly imaginable
        in view of all I asked.

        I'll need no words
        for what I'll say
        when I'm my shadow,

        it will be evident
        by the light I shed
        on where I stood.

To kill but not to harm

        Blue heron & Cooper's hawk wait
        to take the unwary, not offense.
        They try to cast no shadow,
        to kill but not to harm.
        I fly among them like a flicker
        knowing I will wind up
        a pile of feathers on the ground.
        They are not developers,
        the trees are safe with them,
        we are safe with the trees,
        but the predator who waits
        for me to give offense
        casts a long shadow.

Chaos

Simulacra never dance as well
as originals like us. Religion
is about their not knowing it,
but, like homeless veterans, we
suffer from manipulating them.

It's not as if they're puppets;
they're getting wise to us.
At first they thought we were gods,
whole bureaucracies of them,
then they rolled us up into one.

And occasionally it seemed to us
they were thinking for themselves,
becoming limber, inventing
simulations of their own, and we
began to feel competitive.

A failure of our responsibility,
or perhaps a crack in our hubris.
In any case, things went wrong:
we became attracted to them
and they became less like us.

Escaping them

    No matter how fast we turn around
    we can't see what's always there
    because it's in our nature not to see
    messengers following us, or,
    have it your way, call them
    other names—escaping them
    is our secret sacred occupation,
    the rest is loud parade.

    We see their shadows in front of us,
    but when we spin around it's dark.
    Something can be done about that:
    we can track their scents like wolves
    into the taigas of our stories, conflating
    them obscenely until we stumble
    on ourselves and fall asleep chagrined
    as beached sharks.

Consequence aside

> If we could take something with us
> I would take all those glances that said
> save me not from whom or what—
> I would leave all that blather behind,
> I would take the fear and hope
> of a place more merciful than this
> to lay it at the feet of gray-eyed goddesses
> and set consequence aside.

Loss

Peter O'Toole and Eleanor Parker
left this week to vacation
on Chiron or is it Sirius?
I don't travel well, I'm staying
to miss them here awhile,
to help earth adjust to their absence,
but wherever I look black holes
open through which gods go
as if there is no atmosphere left
for us to walk in, so I fly
and pretend I can't as if
we don't traffic in each other
and bear incalculable loss.

Dry bones in their cars

It's not about what so & so will think,
would think, does think, it's about this,
this fathomable celebration
this mind paid into the deep.

How much of it is there to pay?

There is no beyond these intersections
& traffic circles for the dry bones
in their cars shuttered against the seasons
and all their reasons for getting on

or getting over on

ghosts who happily kluge our brains
to revise encounters that we blew
and move on as if we hadn't left
our best friend bleeding in a ditch.

Outfall

> Here in the world of what won't happen again
> we are devoted to again, pitfall by footfall
> in fast reverse we hurtle forward so as not
> to see our squandering of it, that one thing
>> that won't happen again
>> upon which life depends.
>> No matter what we believe again
>> nothing comes again
>> even though it casts a shadow.

As if they had a conscience

> When a bright day hurts like your ill body
> and you know you change what you see
>
> you will be bolder where you look
> as if gods had a conscience
>
> and when history puts you to rest
> you will keep them company.

Infinite ampersand

> Too many of us, too little compassion,
> a jangling press, heartache galore—
> all this under the owl's stare,
> vermin in the night scurrying
> to Walmarts in our disgrace.
>
> Facets of the same jewel.
>
> There should at least be an algorithm
> to check the swoop of time enough
> to let us what, what would we do
> with time enough, in time enough
> to light an eye to warm us, in time
>
> to fete the jewel of quantum physics,
> amplituhedron & infinite ampersand.
>
> Facets of the same jewel.

The full intent of the reckless eye

The earth is bleeding light, we are bleeding light
too bright for eyes occluded by the news,
eyes shaded against inquiry and the full intent
of the reckless eye. Be still, scientists,
I know the eye is made of the same substance
as the brain. My intent is to haunt the corridors.
I know the heart is an organ, not a metaphor
for the senses' witness. I know
your objections to alchemy and say
whatever light strikes casts a shadow,
changing what we see, that's what I'm talking about,
changing that we see and being responsible for it.
Now let the music in you hone the irrational number's edge,
now let the music in you praise the zero's ruthlessness, now bleed
in the name of whatever makes for light.

This life has cut you open.

To catch a lightning bolt

Will anyone's face tic, lips purse
looking at my face when I'm gone?
It only matters now not when
I hear the Milky Way thrum
and remember thistle fondly.
I've seen caged panthers pace
behind a loved one's eyes, seen
vipers lift behind a smile;
I know they cannot be appeased,
to try to appease is to consent
to hoodwinking the child.
I always knew who wished me ill;
illness came of denying it.
The shutter takes a thousandth of a second
to catch a lightning bolt
and so it will be with any of you
whose lips purse to think I'm dead—
none of us are, hard as we try to be.
Why would memory make us nervous
unless we know time whipsaws,
goodbye is hello and flowers
are fewer than our encounters?

Under the bed

I dropped a sweater on the floor,
a piece of it crept away.
I don't believe this any more than you
and yet I testify that room forebodes
brushes with the scent of abandoners.

A creature departed me
and now consorts with long-eyed ones
that, shaking off my judgment,
invite me to cavort
as if we'd never met before.

Death sends ornate invitations
current occupants intercept,
perhaps a feline messenger,
and death is not amused that I
prefer to sleep under the bed.

If one white wing

Bedfellows

If one white wing disappears
when you see me close the door
behind me in the moonlight would
you report me to the IRS or
Homeland Security or the NSA
or would you add it to the list
of securities held in denial
of such ordinary things as
daemons lying next to us
as we rebuild the world
to accommodate our injuries?

I think that one white wing would
blind you to the rest of your life.

Atoms & evenings

The atoms of my body begin
to remember evenings spent
in other civilizations.

Death must be recollection and I
must be a feast of atoms waking
to their biographies

& therefore I'm as many parts
as all my dreams and recognitions
in faces half remembered.

I've seen Alexander pacing
in the periphery of my eye
and Hypatia at her desk.

As with the fragments of a Sappho poem
nothing is lost because we say it is
nor is the author unknown.

We know less about the known
than we think less about the whole,
so much doesn't need a story.

We tell one anyway to explain
the terrible work we refuse to do,
work for which each atom calls.

The heronry

I used to avoid men who looked like me.
I didn't think I could bring them around
    to talk of inconsequential things.

Here's what I made of their hawkish looks,
that they would sit all night on pilings listening
    to the exhalation of deceits.

No one panders to such intent
or breaks the concentration
of one who has no doubts.

Such men cast no shadow
even if the sun insists they do—
I will know when to roll up my own.

Hadrian weeps

My search for the color of Hadrian's eyes
did not match any news results. Try fewer keywords.
Yeah, that will help as much
as suffering the little children to come unto molesters
for which there aren't any synonyms
and not enough opprobrium to go around.

Top hats, crystal flutes,
gonfalons, Hadrian's impulses, kettle drums,
the particular curvature of a wave,
uncountable exactitudes
waiting to reunite us
with that one moment
when we understood
we had to come again.

All our songs are yearning
all our art is burning
for the light this life shades
and sometimes someone sees
its coattail in our eyes.

We must do more for the ancients than gawk
and pose before their statues,
but a world trapped
between shutter and sound byte lost
its reverence for anything, so screaming kids
and their look-at-me moms sack the place
as Vandals did before, and Hadrian weeps

as much for us as for Antinous,
but we're busy being noticed,
leaving our fingerprints on our devices.

Lioness in the rug

>The lioness in the rug studies me
as I should have studied every sense and scent,
studies me with such repose that I regret
the jingle of my pocket full of urgencies
and the ruffling of my hullabaloo.

The chef is full of it

To be so much a part of a place,
then to be gone Sunday afternoon
affirms an insomniac's conviction
something worse is about to happen,
something devoted to you:
someone is always selected for this loss.

Even the dishes speak of it,
the sun burns a little more remorseless,
the clinical stare across the room,
pitiless as acid reflux, says
you cannot rescue the woman
in the corner from her old age;
no one rescued her from her youth.

The look-at-me's soak cannoli shells
with their soggy need. The chef
is full of it, like your mother.

Nothing's going well because someone's
not there, the same someone
absent at your birth. No,
not your mother. She was never there,
but someone who promised you
and was detained, someone
for whom the lost are surrogate,
someone you're now unable to await.

Hurt of golems

He must get in there
or freeze those frames
& come out however changed
or not & in this way
assuage the algorithm
offended by his hubris.

Can he do this can
anyone go back in
to loosen that fixed horror
that deathly grin
of incident stuck
in the plumbing of time?

And do we know where
there is, does anyone
once lightning strikes
& windows rattle &
all that we had hoped
becomes a flight of crows?

We must get in the bone
the wood the marrow—
the danger is to never
break out to join
the frozen ghostly ones
in the gilded frame

& to be an artifact
in an attic subject
to the death of mice,
rummaging of lawyers
inquiring fingers &
inconsolable light.

He owes his conscience
to free the reel
from the ratchets & riots
of ill-considered acts,
damned hurt of golems
& their wicked makers.

Inheritance

It's too cruel to inherit things,
but is it the cruelty of the living
or the dead? Too cruel to muck
the sorrows and shadows
of someone else's memory,
to finger the bent light waves
of desires you have no right to know,
too cruel and corrupting.
Bequeathals curse, inheritances incinerate
in the Saint Elmo's fire of ghostly riggings.
We're all striae and moraine
of one ice age or another,
studied by geologists taking
samples of our cores to study
in some impenetrable privacy.

Riding alligators

Please separate us from our dreams
so that without the helicopters
we may rest in culverts
before riding alligators past
the wired ambitions of men.

Please
deliver us from our makings,
the misadventures of our memories,
so that in purity to say goodbye
we can set out to nowhere in particular
with a reasonable expectation
of getting there as innocent
as we arrived.

Please
not from that place again
but from someplace new
this life we spent to eschew
let us incinerate
so that we may emulate
earth repairing herself.

Cosmos trickling down

The bird in the flue
may crash the economy
of the empire of denial.

It's not the plumber's problem
or the electrician's,
and if not you then who?

You lit the light that drew
the jay to crash the window,
you are the squirrel in the attic,

the bird in the flue
and the broken jay,
cosmos trickling down.

This abandoner of dogs

Hard to brush off heaven,
to need a watch & compass
& language to remember
a place locked out from,
but this abandoner of dogs
& children visits them
when the moon burns a hole
through this thatch of twigs,
this shelter from the past
& this abandoner of dogs,
this liar is sucked out from
sleep & other excuses
to risk life in the mouth
of the scented encompasser,
life not as a passerby
but food for what happens
to the habitable moment
that is not spurned to linger
for another wretched day.

Dusty phones

The mute callers rest
or perhaps they're dead;
what they dared not
stared them down.
Dusty phones reek
of their cowed names
in the attic of my mind;
did they ever learn
what I tried so hard
to learn, that this
thisness of anything
is all there is
and distance is about
positing fears?

Cyberspace

The dead are easier to love than the living
or is that too obvious to say?
We're now more within each other's reach
and have nothing to lose but our lives.
We sense the dead's permission
to fool around with our stories.
What have we to say? They hear us think.
Do they find us tedious? We find them
endlessly fascinating now—we take
anything we want from them.
Are they interested in what we take,
not being diminished by it as they feared
when we slept afoot and lied to them
about what we really wanted? I think
the dead are not compliant but awake
and we must sleep to love them truly.

Old artist

In old age his hands are still
a fireplace to roast his enemies in
but he prefers coals for barefoot memories to walk
or kilns dead dervishes haunt.

They hurt for having lifted so many possibilities
to the wall.

He washes them in forgetful turpentine.

Gerund, goodbye

Trinity of spies

You don't have to be somewhere else,
doing something else. Do nothing here
and give rise to another species.

Get rid of personal pronouns,
that trinity of spies. Do nothing.
When the occasion arises do nothing again.

Be still in the cosmos of zero,
the whiteness of O, the space between
our grand compulsions

from which new worlds arise,
in which decadence subsides, the circuit
where we no longer need identities

and may call ourselves one,
recognitions being merely a fleet resting
in the eye of a storm.

Gerund, goodbye

I

Pirouette elementals
to crackling November's chord, charm my gerunds off,
put them on to keep warm. I give my first person
to you to make of us a gala death of all
but that other we come here to become.

Pirouette to molt self from wintry bones
deluding us to think this moment's not
our destiny and tomorrow
is made of this, this elixir ennobling
the wish to disappear, the will to be at one.

Goodbye gerunds anchoring
verbs that shelter in the eye of storms,
goodbye tails caught underfoot and squealing,
goodbye state and status, pretense goodbye.

Now press the wine from my face
with the gorgeous crush of too much too fast
and drink to your new year. If not mine as if
I had not disturbed your sleep
and I had not awakened
so calamitously. Press the mutiny from my limbs
and hoist the flag of state
as if I had not been anything but a rogue verb.

You rhyme too much, whine too much
& are about ellipses & pretending
to be no otherwhere when I know

you listen only to your own heart beat
& can't hear above the din of it
the roar of mine.

The second person is the first question:
Who are you?

You in whom I am overcome
only to rise in the throat of the question
what are you looking at?
I am looking at you
but you could never look at me.

II

It has taken me eighty years to settle down here
and even then I'm not at home.
I mean by here the planet.

I've a lot to celebrate knowing this,
knowing I got here having little use
for first or third person—
it was always about you
whoever you are,
whoever you are I've followed your scent
and sometimes heard you breathe,
and if there is no reunion
there will be nothing to regret.

III

Somewhere is this you who can stop
a thing from what it portends, stop
the gerund from molesting the verb,
and each life is a longing for that you
which on the other side of things appears
in the holy wordlessness of dreams.

All that makes him laugh

No matter how she plays her violin
the child sounds like a harpsichord,
her klezmer turns to Telemann.

His hallowed notes ennoble
bombast and booze before
they pour into the street.

Ebony and intestine
can't be tuned finely enough
to kill him civilly.

Some other way must be found
to madden him to death,
but first he must be made to laugh

and all that makes him laugh
is the vaudeville dog that won't
jump through his master's hoop.

Wardrobes of Numina

Shorter, hairier, wartier, warier,
disinclined to license death—
the gods had to pay us something
to wear us like their wardrobes;
we should use that money well,
not spending it on the theater
of whiny helplessness and fear
when we know more than we cop to
and own more than we want.

Who gave her permission to die
leaving us to wonder what we said,
permission to die leaving us
slow and humpbacked here,
and who gave us permission to forget
the gods acknowledge their debt
by giving us something to despise,
something divine and dangerous
for us to treat like smelly socks?

Her face

Her face depends upon its flesh
as if the bones were hiding
from the loitering look.
Not that the camera's cruel
but that it's innocent.

Our choices are about aperture
and shutter speed, about
the quality of the lens
and the secrets of what we apprehend.
We are what we choose to see.

Carbon mnemonic

Stone to the camera's eye
so unconcerned with self
light conjugates it &
wears what's on it well—

leaf, sock, condom,
it even tolerates paint,
a carbon mnemonic
of our fortune as stars.

Stone asks does it matter
whatever matters most
and we answer
by turning it to statues

or fences and paving,
then light caresses it
as if we don't matter.
Light is balm against us.

Consent to ash

In old age I look like someone else
someone I ought to be, not
exactly the other or even another
but someone who ought to give a shit
and so obviously doesn't he offends
the projectionist in his booth.

It's about genetics as much as Murnau
thought it explained Nosferatu,
it's more about shadows, lens,
and what remnant innocence invites,
about us as we consent to ash
and what we look forward to then.

The edible curd of a question mark

What to do hello here his hair turned white
and she was as embarrassed by him
as she had been when he was born
so hard to be forty-five with such a son.

Hoo-yi-yay and what not do for all
that consternation about who
belongs to whom when it's a fact
we're lame and sent from the pack

to forage on our own and be shot down
from helicopters in Wyoming
and darker two-legged places
where territorialists dwell,

and if we don't dye our hair
how will world have its comeuppance
and should I honor that remark
with the edible curd of a question mark?

Tag

Where were you before?
Before? Your accident.
I was considering who
my parents ought to be
when someone pushed me
and there I was somewhere
without belongings.
Belongings? Yes,
site-specific senses
needed for reconnaissance.
You were ill-prepared?
Prepared for somewhere else.
To be someone else?
I brought him with me,
an elemental playing tag
with suits and flirts
I took too seriously.
Sensory processing disorder
it's called, I call it
raw material troubled
into art, something
left over from before
the nakba, somewhere
fruits jollied skies
and I had no reason
to envy herons or cry.

Goodbye beasts

The beasts of memory on their hind legs
dance in the blood-dappled forests
through which I crashed alone
enough to be beside myself
without anybody noticing.

Like Doctor Frankenstein, I made them
and must speak to them respectfully
not as children but immigrants
who bring such treasures with them
it will take many years to count them.

Much of me is left in tatters
in bull briar and clutching branches
but what arrives on the beach
is ready for ocean's mortar.
Goodbye dancers, goodbye beasts.

Furnace of red lilies

In the furnace of red lilies
for all the licking of the names
for all they're being kindling would
she feels him looking at her
without pity in the knowledge of
being stripped of worlds
that require them to explain
the this & that of existential pain
when all they really had to do was love

In the furnace of red lilies
they hear each other's true name
& know it was worthwhile
to heed the contrarian who ordered them
to go left when right beguiled
to turn dark corners to make dark quarters home

Fit to walk naked

The furnishings of my imagination,
odor of event, architecture
and trees decay in my sleep;
I awake in operating rooms
more cleansed than the dead,
fit to walk naked in malls
wondering who will see me
and if I will make better decisions then
than when I dressed myself
for occasions yearning to be lost.

The light is too bright

snow is falling mercifully
on the lurid detail
of the citadel of sleep
and before I wake
I pay due respect
to the gods of this place
who play the minor figures
in these conundrums
from which I wake

the light is too bright
the traffic too loud
and you are too big
whoever you are
wherever you are
whatever you signify
but it doesn't matter
because where I truly live
snow is falling mercifully

All he had to say

What is bliss but being punctuated by the wind?

To trees and empty rooms he said
all he had to say, to stones
& passersby, not important men.
They stopped his mouth with gifts
he didn't want. Importance reeked
of grotty fingers & contempt
ripe as soiled underthings.

Who would kill this audience for paper,
punish rooms for bareness,
harangue strangers, cheer pedants?
Have respect, he told the boy
as he pulled him through the knot;
respect what they told you not to think,
suck up to stones, dance with bums,
choose an audience without means.

What is bliss but being interrupted by the wind?

www.ingramcontent.com/pod-product-compliance
Lightning Source LLC
LaVergne TN
LVHW041548070426
835507LV00011B/989